KNOW YOUR SPORT

Golf

Clive Gifford

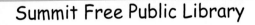

SEA-TO-SEA

Mankato Collingwood London

This edition first published in 2010 by
Sea-to-Sea Publications
Distributed by Black Rabbit Books
P.O. Box 3263, Mankato, Minnesota
56002

Library of Congress Cataloging-in-Publication Data

Gifford, Clive.
   Golf / Clive Gifford.
      p. cm. -- (Know your sport)
   Includes index.
   ISBN 978-1-59771-217-0 (hardcover)
   1. Golf--Juvenile literature. I. Title.
   GV968.G54 2010
   796.352--dc22
                                        2008045861

9 8 7 6 5 4 3 2

Published by arrangement with the Watts
Publishing Group Ltd., London

Series editor: Jeremy Smith
Art director: Jonathan Hair
Series designed and created for
Franklin Watts by Storeybooks.
Designer: Rita Storey
Editor: Nicola Edwards
Photography: Tudor Photography,
   Banbury

Note: At the time of going to press, the statistics
and player profiles in this book were up to date.
However, due to some players' active
participation in the sport, it is possible that some
of these may now be out of date.

Picture credits
© Shaun Best/Reuters/Corbis p7, © Jon Hrusa/
epa/Corbis p13(bottom), © Ron Kuntz/
Reuters/Corbis p19(bottom), © Bettmann/
CORBIS p23(top); istock pp 4 and 8.

Every attempt has been made to clear copyright.
Should there be any inadvertent omission please
apply to the publisher for rectification.

Cover images: Tudor Photography, Banbury.

All photos posed by models.
Thanks to Katherine O'Connor, Bati Mupasi, and
Richard Whiston.

The Publisher would like to thank Tadmarton
Heath Golf Club and coach Tom Jones for all
their help.

All the players shown in this book are right-
handed but golf can be played by left-handed
players equipped with suitable left-handed clubs.

Taking part in sports
is a fun way to get in shape, but
like any form of physical
exercise it has an element of
risk, particularly if you are unfit,
overweight, or suffer from any
medical conditions. It is
advisable to consult a healthcare
professional before beginning
any program
of exercise.

Contents

What is Golf?

Golf is one of the oldest and most popular ball sports in the world. Players use a club to strike a small golf ball. Play takes place on a golf course made up of nine or 18 holes. On each hole, a player aims to hit the fewest number of shots to get the ball from the start of the hole into a small, 4.2-in (10.8-cm) diameter cup, marked by a flag.

Power and Skill

Today's players can take advantage of the latest technology in clubs and balls but they also need to be excellent athletes. Top golfers can strike the ball well over 820 feet (250m) with a single shot, yet power is only part of the sport. Incredible skill and technique are required for each shot to be accurate and concentration has to be intense over the three hours or so it takes to complete all 18 holes.

A golf ball weighs no more than 1.6 ounces (45.9g). Its tough outer surface is covered in dimples. Always try to use a ball without splits in the casing and carry plenty of spares with you.

This player starts play on a golf hole by hitting her first shot, called a drive. This shot is played from the tee area. The other players stay quiet and watch her shot.

The History of Golf

Golf developed out of various stick and ball games in Europe, but its spiritual home is Scotland in the fourteenth and fifteenth centuries. It became so popular that many men neglected their archery training as soldiers to play it and special laws had to be passed. The first golf association, formed in 1744, was based at St. Andrews in Scotland. This became the Royal and Ancient (R&A) in 1834 which, along with the United States Golf Association (USGA), now runs the rules of the game. Golf was a sport only for the very wealthy until the twentieth century when it began spreading throughout the world. Now, everyone can join in the fun.

Scotland's Colin Montgomerie plays a shot at the 2004 Masters competition in Augusta, Georgia. The Masters is one of four prestigious events held each year known as the Majors. The other three are the Open Championship, the U.S. Open, and the PGA Championship.

Professional Golf

Professional golfers compete on tours with different events every week. Most events are played over four rounds of golf featuring 72 holes. The scoring system for nearly all of these tournaments is called strokeplay. Each player's total number of shots taken over all 72 holes plus any penalty strokes (see page 18) are added together and the player with the lowest total score wins. Golf is mainly an individual sport but there are some team competitions. The most famous are the Ryder Cup for men and the Solheim Cup for women, both of which pit a European team against a team from the United States.

Junior Golf

You're never too young to start playing golf. Tiger Woods was only three years old when he completed nine holes in just 48 shots! Good junior golfers play on full golf courses and can take part in competitions. Many beginners though, start their golf career at other locations. Park putting greens and local driving ranges allow young players to play shots and practice their golf swing. Pitch and Putt courses are great fun and highly recommended for beginners. The holes tend to be much shorter than on a full golf course, but are still a stiff test with hazards to avoid.

The Golf Course

A golf course is made up of a series of individual holes, usually 18 holes though many nine-hole courses exist. The term "a round of golf" is considered to mean 18 holes.

Course Features

All the holes on a golf course are different but they share certain features. Each hole starts with one or more flat tee areas. Players have to take their shot in between and behind a pair of tee markers on the tee. Markers for junior players are often further up the hole, making the hole shorter and a little easier.

Ahead of the tee is a corridor of short, mown grass called the fairway. To the left and right of the fairway there may be areas of long grass called the rough and sometimes rows of bushes and trees. Hazards such as sand-filled depressions called bunkers and streams can cross the fairway. Ahead of the fairway is the green. This is an area of carefully prepared grass in which the actual hole or cup is located. The position of the hole is marked by a flagpole 6ft 6in (2m) high with a flag on top. Golfers play a hole in a group of up to four players. After they have all played their first shot, the player to play next is usually the golfer whose ball is farthest from the flag.

Handicaps

Players who play regularly at a golf club can get a handicap. This can be a number from 0 to 36, which is the number of shots more than the par a golfer tends to take to complete the course. Handicaps are used in competitions between amateur golfers.

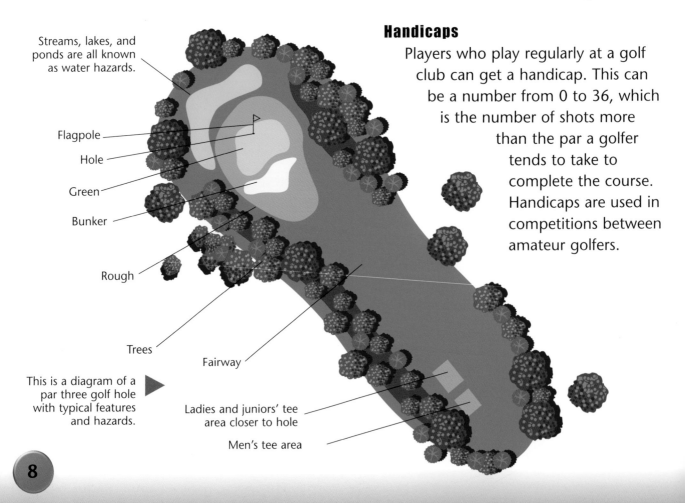

Streams, lakes, and ponds are all known as water hazards.

Flagpole

Hole

Green

Bunker

Rough

Trees

Fairway

This is a diagram of a par three golf hole with typical features and hazards.

Ladies and juniors' tee area closer to hole

Men's tee area

Players write down their score on a scorecard after finishing a hole. Players must never cheat or miscount their score or they will be disqualified.

Good golfers always respect the course they're playing on by not leaving litter behind and by repairing any damage their shots make. Here, a player replaces a divot (a loose piece of turf) back in the fairway, pressing it down firmly.

When one player's ball is on the green, he or she may ask another player to "attend the flag." The second player holds the flag still and removes it from the hole as the ball rolls toward it.

Par for the Course

Holes vary in length and complexity. Holes are measured in yards and the shortest tend to be 100 yards upward, while the longest are 500 yards or more. Each hole has a par score—usually either of three, four, or five—to indicate its length or difficulty. If you take five shots on a par five hole, for instance, you have made par. The different names for scores above and below par are given below. The par for the course is the par scores for all 18 holes added together. Many full golf courses have a par of 70 or 72.

Above and Below Par for a Hole

Two shots over par = a Double Bogey
One shot over par = a Bogey
One shot under par = a Birdie
Two shots under par = an Eagle
Three shots under par = an Albatross

Equipment and Etiquette

A golfer's equipment includes clothing, a supply of golf balls, and up to 14 clubs. This is all stored in a golf bag, which is carried on the shoulder between shots or, at some courses, attached to a wheeled cart or carried for the player by a person called a caddie.

The different amounts of angle, called loft, on four clubs: 3 wood, 3 iron, 6/7 iron, and a sand wedge. The smaller the number of a club, the less loft on the blade of the club. This means that, if the ball is hit well, it will travel lower and farther.

Golf Clubs

All golfers carry a club called a putter, which is used on and around the green. The other clubs, called woods and irons, are usually numbered, such as a 7 iron or a 2 wood. The exceptions are the pitching and sand wedge clubs, which are used in bunkers and close to the green. Clubs are available for left-handed or right-handed players and come in different lengths for junior players.

Adult clubs can sometimes be cut down to suit smaller players as well. A new full set of golf clubs can be very expensive, but when starting out you only need a handful of clubs: one wood, a long iron (such as a 3 or 4 iron) a mid-range iron (such as a 6 or 7 iron), a lofted iron (such as a wedge), and a

This player's lightweight bag contains his clubs as well as an umbrella, a scorecard and pencil, and a bottle of juice or water.

This young player is wearing a long-sleeved polo shirt and comfortable slacks.

Rubber grip

Shaft

Club face is where you strike the ball.

Grooves in club face should be clean.

Club head

putter. These can often be obtained cheaply secondhand either at golf retailers or even swap meets and yard sales. Take an experienced golfer with you to check on the clubs' condition.

Golf Clothing

Many golf courses have rules about what young players can and cannot wear, so always ask beforehand. Good clothing for golf should be comfortable so as not to restrict your swing, but not so baggy that the clothing gets in the way. Players need to be prepared for all weather conditions, so a sweater, hat, and lightweight set of waterproof pants and jacket are useful, as are a baseball cap and sun block in sunnier weather.

Shoes and Gloves

More and more golf courses are allowing young players to play with flat soled running shoes, but if you're serious about playing you will eventually want a pair of golf shoes. These are fitted with molded plastic bumps or metal spikes that offer grip without damaging the course. A golf glove is worn on the left hand if you are right-handed and on the right if you are left-handed. Usually made of thin leather, the glove helps with your grip and should fit snugly without having wrinkles.

Etiquette

How to act and behave correctly on a golf course is known as etiquette. This may sound stuffy, but etiquette helps games of golf run quickly, smoothly, and safely. It includes avoiding any delays and helping other players by keeping quiet and still as they take their shots and watching the ball to see where it lands. Always wait for the way ahead to be clear on a hole before making a shot.

This golfer is searching for his ball and waves golfers behind him through so as not to hold them up.

This golfer shouts "Fore!" after accidentally hitting the ball toward another fairway. This alerts other golfers to watch out for the ball.

Getting Started

Getting started begins with learning how to grip a golf club and how to line yourself and the club up with the ball before you play a shot. This latter set of actions is known as addressing the ball.

Grips

There are a number of different golf grips. Here we show the interlocking grip, but your golf coach may recommend a different form of grip. The key is to remember that, even though it is called a grip, you shouldn't clench the club so tightly that your knuckles turn white. The grip should keep the club under control without tensing your hands or wrists. It will feel strange at first, but you will get used to it quickly.

Grip Checks

Check the V-shape made by your thumb and first finger of each hand in your grip.

For a right-handed player, the right hand V-shape should point to your right shoulder. The left should point to your right ear.

Addressing the Ball

Grip the club properly and approach the ball. Move the club into position behind the ball, carefully letting the club's base sit on the ground. If you nudge the ball forward, it

The Interlocking Grip

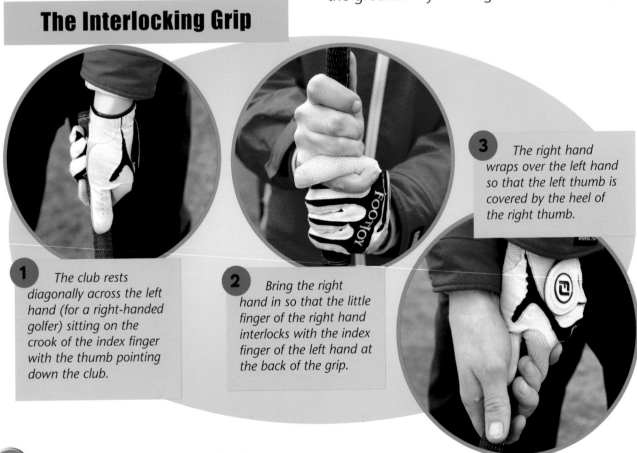

1 The club rests diagonally across the left hand (for a right-handed golfer) sitting on the crook of the index finger with the thumb pointing down the club.

2 Bring the right hand in so that the little finger of the right hand interlocks with the index finger of the left hand at the back of the grip.

3 The right hand wraps over the left hand so that the left thumb is covered by the heel of the right thumb.

This player is addressing the ball in a good, balanced stance. He aims to keep his shoulders and arms relaxed with his arms hanging close to the body before starting his swing.

Eyes down, looking at the back of the ball but with chin not tucked in.

Lean from the waist, keeping a straight back.

Knees flexed comfortably

Right shoulder a little lower as right hand lower on club.

Ball in between both feet for shorter irons (6-9). For longer irons and wood, ball should be closer to your front foot, the left foot for a right-handed player.

Club face behind ball and square to the ball.

The takeaway is the very start of the backswing. It begins with the shoulders turning. Your wrists should stay straight as your shoulders, body, and arms begin to turn. Your head should remain still and always looking at the ball.

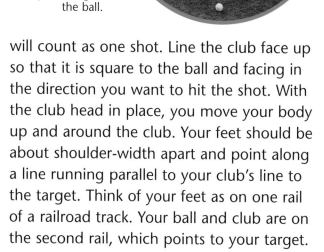

will count as one shot. Line the club face up so that it is square to the ball and facing in the direction you want to hit the shot. With the club head in place, you move your body up and around the club. Your feet should be about shoulder-width apart and point along a line running parallel to your club's line to the target. Think of your feet as on one rail of a railroad track. Your ball and club are on the second rail, which points to your target.

Annika Sorenstam

Date of Birth: October 9th, 1970

Nationality: Swedish

Height: 5 ft 6 in (1.68m)

Right-Handed

Total Tournament Wins: 90

Major Wins: 10

Currently the world's most successful female golfer, Annika burst onto the LPGA scene in the mid-1990s. She has notched up an incredible 69 LPGA tournament victories, including 10 majors, and has been Rolex Player of the Year a record eight times. In 2003, she made history by being the first woman since 1945 to play in a men's PGA tournament. In 2001, she also became the first female player to record a score of 59 for a round in any LPGA tournament.

Annika Sorenstam about to play the first shot on a hole during practice in South Africa. Her club is at the top of its backswing, parallel with the ground and with an almost straight left arm.

13

The Swing

The regular golf swing is a smooth, rhythmic, circular-shaped swing of the golf club. Although the swing can be divided into three parts—the backswing, downswing, and follow-through—it is made as one continuous, flowing movement.

Building Your Swing

For absolute beginners, a coach may suggest players only perform a half swing, with the club just going past the horizontal on the backswing and the follow-through. As you get more comfortable with this half swing, you can lengthen your backswing. Think of your swing as a winding up of a giant spring. You need to coil the energy up

The Swing

Club pointing to target.

Left shoulder turning.

1 The player has completed the club takeaway. As the club reaches a horizontal position, he starts to cock (bend) the wrists upward. As the hips begin to turn, the player's body weight starts to shift to over his back foot.

2 The hips and shoulders keep turning to take the club back. At the top of the full backswing, the club shaft will be parallel to the ground with your back facing the target. Most of the player's weight is now over his front foot.

3 The player starts to uncoil on the downswing with the body turning and weight transferring from his front to his back leg. The player's shoulders pull his arms and hands down with the club coming last. The movement is made naturally without the player trying to force the club down fast.

in a slow, accurate backswing so that you can uncoil on the downswing and follow-through to generate power but with balance and control.

Nelson's Record Number

American golfer Byron Nelson (1912–2006) had an amazing year in 1945. He won 11 tournaments in a row and 18 tournaments in total, a record to this day.

Club face hits ball square.

Right heel comes off ground to allow player to turn.

4 *As the downswing continues, the player uncocks his wrists. A good swing sees the club make a clean, crisp impact with the back of the ball at the very bottom of the swing. The head stays down with the eyes focused on where the ball was.*

5 *The player swings through the ball. The loft on the club head lifts the ball up and into the air. The golfer's hips continue to turn after impact as the club rises on its follow-through.*

6 *The player cocks his wrists as the club follows through past the horizontal. His head swivels so that it is over the right shoulder. The club travels over his left shoulder as he turns with his chest facing the target. He tries to hold the finish position for several seconds as he watches the flight of his ball.*

Don't expect your first attempts at swinging the club to be 100 percent successful. It takes a lot of hard work and an equally large amount of patience to build a good, accurate swing that you can repeat time and time again.

This player strikes the ball cleanly. This is the result of many hours of practice with every shot taken seriously.

Taking Lessons

The very best way to learn and improve your golf game is to have a series of golf lessons with a qualified teacher or professional golfer. A good teacher can take you through your stance, alignment, and swing and notice things you cannot see or feel yourself. He or she can set you "homework" drills and exercises for you to practice, so you can work on your game in between lessons. Group lessons, where a number of junior golfers are instructed by one teacher or coach, can be really good value.

Practice Makes Perfect

Your golf teacher or coach is best placed to suggest ideal practice drills for you and your abilities. You cannot practice golf shots in most parks or open land unless you have definite permission. If you have a small lawn, a piece of thick carpet (a minimum of a yard by half a yard in size) to protect the grass allows you to practice your swing without using a ball. You should aim to just brush the carpet with the bottom of the club on the way through. If you have access to a larger area of ground, buy a set of cheap air flow balls made of plastic and full of holes. These balls are designed for practice because they don't travel that far. Take every practice shot as seriously as you would a regular shot.

A professional golf coach takes three junior players through their stance and alignment when addressing the ball. Following your golf coach's instructions and practice ideas can result in a real improvement in your game.

Driving Ranges

A driving range is an especially useful place for practicing golf shots with real golf balls. For a small fee, players receive a large bucket of balls that they can hit without having to retrieve them afterward. Make sure that you concentrate and take your time over each ball. Don't get into the habit of banging through a basket of balls without thinking about each shot.

Common Faults

There are many different faults that can occur. Many are the result of an incorrect grip or not lining yourself up correctly when addressing the ball. Others happen because of the swing not resulting in the club face reaching the ball squarely. It can be hard for a beginner to diagnose what is going wrong, which is where a professional golf teacher can be invaluable.

One of the most common problems for beginners is the tendency to become tense after a series of poor shots. This can result in even more problems, such as speeding up the whole swing to try to force the ball away. If you're struggling with shots, check your grip and how you are addressing the ball thoroughly and try to slow your entire swing down.

A problems that beginners often experience is topping the ball (hitting or skimming the top of the ball). Common reasons for this are lifting your head and with it your body and club during the swing, and not connecting with the ball at the bottom of the swing.

Standing too close to the ball at the address position can result in you shanking the ball. This will send the ball in a direction away from your target line.

This player has lost control of his swing, losing his balance and swiveling round. As a result, he misses the ball. Common causes are too fast a backswing or trying to force the club down on its downswing.

A weak grip with only one knuckle visible can lead to the club face opening (which means turning away from you). This can result in your shot being sliced with the ball veering sharply to the right.

Each hole begins with a drive off the tee area. If golfers are playing together in a group, the player who scored the lowest on the previous hole has what is called "the honor"—and plays the first shot. On the very first hole of a round, players may toss a coin for who has the honor.

Teeing Off Tactics

The first shot on a hole is crucial, so golfers have to think through the options, choosing which club to use—often a long iron or wood for greater distance—and working out where they want to play the ball and how far they want it to travel. Sometimes, bunkers or water hazards across the fairway mean that golfers choose to "lay up," playing a shot shorter than their maximum distance so that they avoid the hazard

and have a good position for their next shot. For the first shot on a hole, players can use a plastic or wooden tee, which raises the ball up off the ground a little.

Provisional Ball

If you fear your shot off the tee might be lost or out of bounds, you are allowed to play a second shot, called a provisional ball, off the tee. If the original ball is not found within five minutes, then the provisional ball becomes the ball in play and your score adds the original shot plus the penalty shot. This, in effect, means that the second time you hit the provisional ball it will be your fourth shot.

Teeing up the ball before making a drive. Take advice from a golf teacher on how high you should tee up the ball. In general, the less loft on a club, the higher you should tee up the ball.

This player drives off the tee. The ball is placed nearer his front foot than back foot. His feet are widely spaced apart. He uses his regular swing and does not try to force or overhit the ball. After the club has swung through the ball, the club follows through and ends up with a high follow-through. The player tries to hold this position for as long as possible.

Fairway Play

A regular swing is used for shots on the fairway. Most players starting out use irons on the fairway, because they offer a little more control than woods. Irons can be divided into long irons (2, 3, and 4 irons), medium irons (5, 6, and 7) and short irons (8, 9, and wedges). The smaller the number iron, the less loft on its club head and the longer the club is. This means that players have to adjust their stance and distance away from the ball.

This player sets his stance for three different clubs—a short iron, a long iron, and a 2 wood. The longer the club, the slightly farther away a player needs to stand to produce a good, free swing.

Tiger Woods

Date of Birth: December 30th, 1975

Nationality: American

Height: 6 ft 1 in (1.85m)

Right-handed

Total Tournament Wins: 85

Major Wins: 14

Eldrick "Tiger" Woods was a golfing child prodigy, playing shots when he was just two years old and winning the Optimist International Junior Championship at the age of only eight. As an adult, Tiger has become one of the most accurate and long hitters off the tee and on the fairway. His consistency and control made him the youngest world number one ranked golfer at 21, smashing the record by eight years. Rarely away from the leaderboard, Tiger's record of major wins is second only to that of Jack Nicklaus, who he seems likely to overtake in the near future.

Pitch and Chip Shots

Sometimes, you may need a full swing with a long or medium iron for your shot to reach the green. Other times, you will be closer and can use either a pitch or a chip shot to get the ball as close to the flag as possible.

Shot Selection

As with all shots, you have to know the typical shot distance you can achieve with a certain club. This only comes with experience and lots of practice. A 7 iron is a typical club used for a chip shot and a

pitching wedge for a pitch shot, but you can experiment with the exact same swing and different clubs to see the different lengths of shot produced.

The Pitch Shot

A pitch shot sends the ball high into the air with the ball not traveling far after landing. Apart from trying to send the ball as near to the hole as possible, you can also use it to get the ball over a hazard, such as bushes or trees, and back farther up on the fairway. For shorter distance pitches, simply shorten the amount of backswing.

The Pitch Shot

1 *With a slightly more narrow stance than usual, address the ball in the center or just behind the center of your stance with your hands slightly ahead of the ball. Take the club back.*

2 *Use a shorter backswing (between half and three-quarters). Let your shoulders turn as normal but your hands should reach shoulder height at most. Let the club swing through the ball at speed.*

3 *Don't try to scoop the ball up by leaning back, let the angle of the club face do that job. Make sure you keep your head down after impact. Your follow-through will see the clubhead rise above shoulder height.*

The Chip Shot

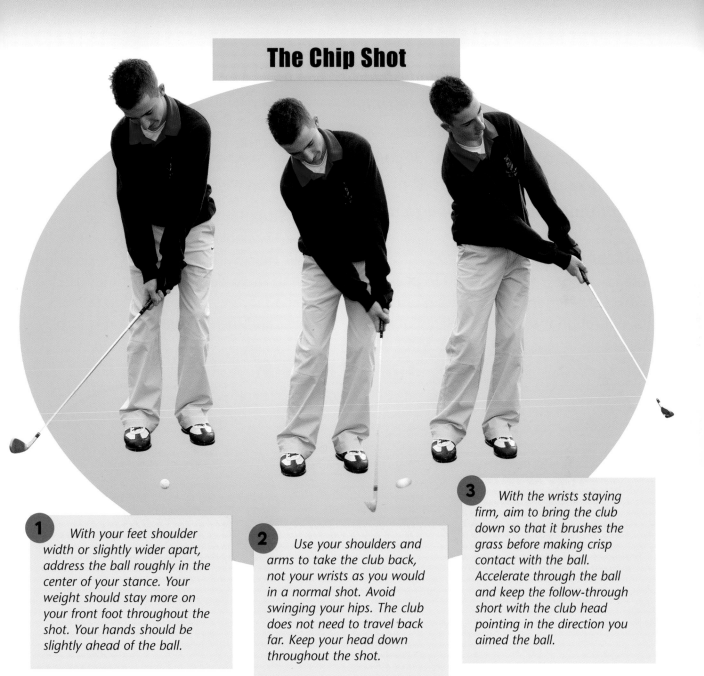

1 With your feet shoulder width or slightly wider apart, address the ball roughly in the center of your stance. Your weight should stay more on your front foot throughout the shot. Your hands should be slightly ahead of the ball.

2 Use your shoulders and arms to take the club back, not your wrists as you would in a normal shot. Avoid swinging your hips. The club does not need to travel back far. Keep your head down throughout the shot.

3 With the wrists staying firm, aim to bring the club down so that it brushes the grass before making crisp contact with the ball. Accelerate through the ball and keep the follow-through short with the club head pointing in the direction you aimed the ball.

The Chip Shot

A chip shot lets the ball fly for a short time in the air before bouncing forward and rolling on. It is used when there are no hazards or obstructions between you and the flag. A chip shot is also sometimes used to play the ball low underneath tree branches when trying to get the ball out of trouble and back on the fairway.

With a chip shot, you are aiming for the ball to land just on the green with its first bounce.

Longest Hole

The Chocolay Downs golf course in Michigan claims to have the longest hole in golf—a par 6 1,007-yard monster!

Bunkers

Lurking along the fairway and often clustered around the green of both full and pitch and putt golf courses, bunkers are a major hazard. If your ball enters a bunker, you need a skillful shot to get it out and clear.

The Sand Wedge

A sand wedge is the ideal club to play short bunker shots as it has a weighted bottom to drive through the sand and plenty of loft to pop the ball up. If you don't have a sand wedge, a pitching wedge or your most lofted club is the next best bet. Your club must not touch the sand when you address the ball. Keep it lifted just above the sand as you line up your shot.

Sand Situations

Not every bunker shot you face will be the same. The splash shot is ideal for situations close to the green. It is sometimes used when a player is stuck in a deep fairway bunker and the only safe option is to play

The Splash Shot

1 *Wriggle your feet into the sand to get a good, firm base with your feet pointing a little left of your target. The club face should be a little open (pointing to the right) about an inch (2-3cm) behind the ball and not touching the sand. Begin your backswing.*

2 *With your weight a little more on your left leg, use a full, slow backswing or, if close to the flag in a shallow bunker, a shorter pitching swing. Bring the club head down at good speed. Aim for the club to first touch the sand about an inch (2-3cm) behind the ball.*

3 *Try to keep your club speed up through the sand and don't lean back. The club should drive through the sand and its loft should send the ball up into the air. Make sure you follow through with a small turn of your hips.*

Severiano Ballesteros

Date of Birth: April 9th, 1957

Nationality: Spanish

Height: 6 ft (1.83m)

Right-Handed

Total Tournament Wins: 94

Major Wins: 5

The most exciting player of his era, Seve stunned the world of golf by coming second and nearly winning the 1976 Open Championship at the tender age of 19. Possessing a magical touch around the greens and bunkers, Seve could sometimes be wayward off the tee but fashioned many incredible recovery shots. He played a massive part in boosting Europe's Ryder Cup fortunes, playing in three winning sides and captaining a fourth side to victory in 1997. He retired in 2007.

Severiano Ballesteros makes a textbook splash shot from a bunker close to the green.

Always rake the sand clear of your shot and footprints after playing a shot. You should also always enter and leave a bunker from its lowest side, rather than climb up its steep face.

A lie every golfer dreads, where the ball is plugged in the sand, is called the fried egg. Keep the clubface square to the ball and use a shorter backswing to punch through the sand (about ½ inch [1cm] behind the ball) and the ball.

the ball out to the side. You can vary how far the ball travels with the splash shot in two ways—shortening or lengthening your swing or aiming to take more or less sand away with the ball during the shot.

If your ball is sitting up well in a shallow fairway bunker you can use a club such as a 7 iron or an 8 iron to hit the ball up the fairway ahead. Sometimes, you will suffer a terrible lie, when your ball is plugged deep in the sand or resting close to the lip of a bunker. In these situations, you should simply aim to get the ball out of the sand on your first attempt.

Course Management and Hazards

A golf course poses many challenges to a player, hole by hole. Good golfers learn to think their way around a golf course, choosing their shots carefully and understanding what they can and cannot do on a particular hole. They should also know the rules when their ball gets into trouble.

Course Management

Whether playing on a putting green, pitch and putt course, or full golf course, your aim is get around the course taking as few shots as possible. Sometimes, this means judging your shot carefully and hitting it well within your maximum distance to make sure your ball avoids a hazard. On other occasions, you may decide to be aggressive and go for a difficult shot. If you do, you have to take the consequences if the shot goes wrong and leaves you in a hazard or in trouble.

Play it as it Lies

A key rule of golf is that you must play your ball as it lies. This means that if it rolls into trouble, such as in thick rough or behind some trees, you have to play it from there. If you decide that your ball is truly unplayable, then you add one shot to your score and can drop the ball two club lengths away from its original lie but not nearer the hole. If your ball lands in a stream or pond, you can play it where it lies or add a shot to your score and drop the ball before the hazard but in line with your original shot. Exceptions to the "play as it lies" rule include what to do if your ball lands in an area of ground that is under repair. In this case, a free drop can be taken one club length away from the area.

This player makes a drop, standing up straight and with the ball at arm's length and shoulder height. The ball may have to be redropped for many reasons, including if it rolls nearer the hole or on to ground under repair.

This player uses his 2 wood, the longest club in his bag, to measure two club lengths away from a tree before dropping his ball.

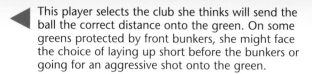

This player selects the club she thinks will send the ball the correct distance onto the green. On some greens protected by front bunkers, she might face the choice of laying up short before the bunkers or going for an aggressive shot onto the green.

In heavy rough and with a bush blocking the path forward, this golfer plays his ball out sideways back onto the fairway. If your ball is in short grass but there are low branches ahead, consider a chip shot with a 3 or 4 iron to keep the ball low.

For a ball lying on a slope above you, try to use a more upright stance and grip farther down the club. Address the ball in the center of your stance and keep your legs steady to avoid leaning back.

Dealing with Difficulty

When in trouble, don't be too ambitious with recovery shots—otherwise you may find that one shot lost becomes two or three. Sometimes, when in heavy rough, for example, it is better to choose a lofted club and get the ball out to the side or a short distance up the fairway rather than go for an epic shot that lands you in deeper trouble.

Even if you keep the ball on the fairway and away from major hazards, you may have to deal with a tough lie, such as a steep slope or your ball sitting in a hole left by an unreplaced divot (see page 9). In this latter case, use an iron with plenty of loft and make sure you get a clean contact to send the ball out of the divot and down the fairway. Some fairways have steep slopes. To play a shot on a steep upward slope, get as much weight as you can on your front foot to avoid leaning back. The slope adds to the loft of the club so you can afford to use a longer iron.

On the Green

Once your ball is on or around the edge of the green, you are likely to reach for your putter and attempt to putt the ball into the hole. Putting is the most crucial part of your game and the time when many shots can be added or cut from your score. Practice putting as often as you can.

Green Rules and Etiquette

Be aware of the position of another player's ball, and never tread on the line between their ball and the hole.

- Don't take practice putts on the green during a round.
- Never jump, run, or hit your club on the green.
- Have the flag attended (see page 9) or take the flag out and well clear when making a putt. If your putt hits the flagpole lying on the green, you incur a penalty of two shots. The player farthest away from the hole is usually the one to putt first.

Putting

1 *This player is lining up a putt. She places the putter behind the ball square to the direction she wants to hit the ball. She bends from the bottom of her back to lean over the ball so that her head is directly above the golf ball.*

2 *Without moving her head, the player takes her putter back. The putting action back and forth is a smooth, continuous movement, a lot like the swinging pendulum on a grandfather clock. No other part of the player's body moves as the putt is made.*

3 *The putter is brought through to hit the ball smoothly without any jerkiness. The player follows through with her putter pointing toward the target. She keeps his head down throughout the stroke.*

Reading the Green

Greens usually contain slopes. If your ball's route to the hole is flat then you can aim it directly at the hole, but if there's a slope you will have to aim above the hole to allow for the slope. If another player has a similar putt to you, watch carefully how the ball moves. This is called "going to school" and can be a useful aid for your own putt. Apart from the exact line you want to send the ball on, you must also judge how much force or strength you want to putt with. This can be adjusted by how far you take the putter back on its

Putting practice is essential to perfect your stroke and to learn with how much force you need to hit a ball. Practice as often as you can.

backswing. Judging the strength of putt is vital. Give the ball a chance of reaching the hole without traveling too far past it.

Holing Out

Even if your ball is fewer than 8 inches (20cm) from the hole, set yourself up for the putt as seriously as for a long-distance birdie attempt. Never try to knock the ball into the hole one-handed. A missed putt from 4 inches (10cm) counts as one shot, just as a drive 650 feet (200m) drive does.

Always make sure that your putter hits the whole of the ball. Many scuffed putts are caused by players lifting their head and with it their putter as they make the shot.

When your ball is in the way of another player's putt or if you want to clean it before putting, place your marker behind the ball carefully and then lift the ball away. The ball must be replaced in exactly the same position.

If your ball leaves a small dent in the green when it lands, repair this with a pronged pitch repairer to raise the grass up to the normal level.

Statistics and Records

Ryder Cup Recent Winners

2008 United States
2006 Europe
2004 Europe
2002 Europe
1999 United States
1997 Europe
1995 Europe
1993 United States
1991 United States

Solheim Cup Recent Winners

2007 United States
2005 United States
2003 Europe
2002 United States
2000 Europe
1998 United States
1996 United States
1994 United States
1992 Europe
1990 United States

Recent Major Winners (Men's)

	The Masters	The U.S. Open	The Open Championship	The PGA
2008	Trevor Immelman	Tiger Woods	Pádraig Harrington	Pádraig Harrington
2007	Zach Johnson	Ángel Cabrera	Pádraig Harrington	Tiger Woods
2006	Phil Mickelson	Geoff Ogilvy	Tiger Woods	Tiger Woods
2005	Tiger Woods	Michael Campbell	Tiger Woods	Phil Mickelson
2004	Phil Mickelson	Retief Goosen	Todd Hamilton	Vijay Singh
2003	Mike Weir	Jim Furyk	Ben Curtis	Shaun Micheel
2002	Tiger Woods	Tiger Woods	Ernie Els	Rich Beem
2001	Tiger Woods	Retief Goosen	David Duval	David Toms
2000	Vijay Singh	Tiger Woods	Tiger Woods	Tiger Woods

Recent Major Winners (Women's)

	Kraft Nabisco Championship	LPGA Championship	U.S. Open	British Open
2008	Lorana Ochoa	Yani Tseng	Inbee Park	Ji-Yai Shin
2007	Morgan Pressel	Suzann Pettersen	Cristie Kerr	Lorena Ochoa
2006	Karrie Webb	Se Ri Pak	Annika Sorenstam	Sherri Steinhauer
2005	Annika Sorenstam	Annika Sorenstam	Birdie Kim	Jeong Jang
2004	Grace Park	Annika Sorenstam	Meg Mallon	Karen Stupples
2003	Patricia Meunier-Lebouc	Annika Sorenstam	Hilary Lunke	Annika Sorenstam
2002	Annika Sorenstam	Se Ri Pak	Juli Inkster	Karrie Webb

Most Major Championships Won

Men
Jack Nicklaus—18
Tiger Woods—14
Walter Hagen—11
Ben Hogan—9
Gary Player—9

Women
Patty Berg—15
Mickey Wright—13
Louise Suggs—11
Annika Sorenstam—10
Babe Zaharias—10

Fewest Shots Taken to Complete a Professional Round on the PGA Tour

59 on a 72 par course by Al Geiberger (1977), Chip Beck (1991), and David Duval (1999).

Longest Drive in PGA Tournament History

427 yards by Chris Smith (1999 Honda Classic)

Glossary and Websites

Approach A shot hit aiming for the green.

Birdie Finishing a hole one shot under par.

Bogey Finishing a hole one shot over par.

Bunker A depression on the course filled with sand.

Caddie A person who carries a player's bag of clubs.

Chip A short shot normally onto the green.

Divot A piece of turf torn out of the ground by a shot, which must always be replaced.

Eagle Finishing a hole two under par.

Etiquette Good behavior and consideration for other golfers and the course.

Fairway The cut grass between the tee and the green.

Hazards Features of a golf course such as bunkers, ditches, a stream, or lake, which make the course more challenging.

Par The number of shots (usually three, four, or five) that it is judged a hole should be completed in by a skilled player.

Professional To be paid to play golf, either through appearance fees, by winning prize money at tournaments, or by being sponsored by companies.

Putt A shot usually made on the green or close to it, where the ball is rolled along the ground using the putter.

Round The word used for playing all the holes in a course.

Tee The rectangular area at the start of a golf hole from where players make their first shot, or drive.

Websites

www.usga.org
The United States Golf Association is the national governing body of golf for the USA, its territories, and Mexico. It was formed in 1894. A non-profit organization, it is run by golfers for the benefit of everyone who plays the game.

www.randa.org
Home of the Royal & Ancient Order of St. Andrews, the R&A, administers the rules of golf in Britain. You can order a free copy of their etiquette guide for young golfers.

www.europeantour.com
The official website of the PGA European Tour, this website has news, photos, videos, and features from tour events and Ryder Cups.

www.lpga.com
Home on the internet of the Ladies PGA tour. The site contains features on the top players, tournaments, and golf tips.

www.rydercup.com
The website for the Ryder Cup. In 34 international matches over the past 77 years, the best American professionals have competed against the best of Great Britain.

http://nytimes.com
Visit the *New York Times* home page and click on Sports, then click on Golf. Here you can read Golf Roundup and Golf Notebook, along with other current stories about golf, as well as keep track of the results and schedules of golf tournaments such as the PGA Tour, The Masters, the U.S. Open, and others. You can also watch video footage of golf.

Note to parents and teachers: every effort has been made by the Publishers to ensure that these websites are suitable for children, that they are of the highest educational value, and that they contain no inappropriate or offensive material. However, because of the nature of the Internet, it is impossible to guarantee that the contents of these sites will not be altered. We strongly advise that Internet access be supervised by a responsible adult.

Index